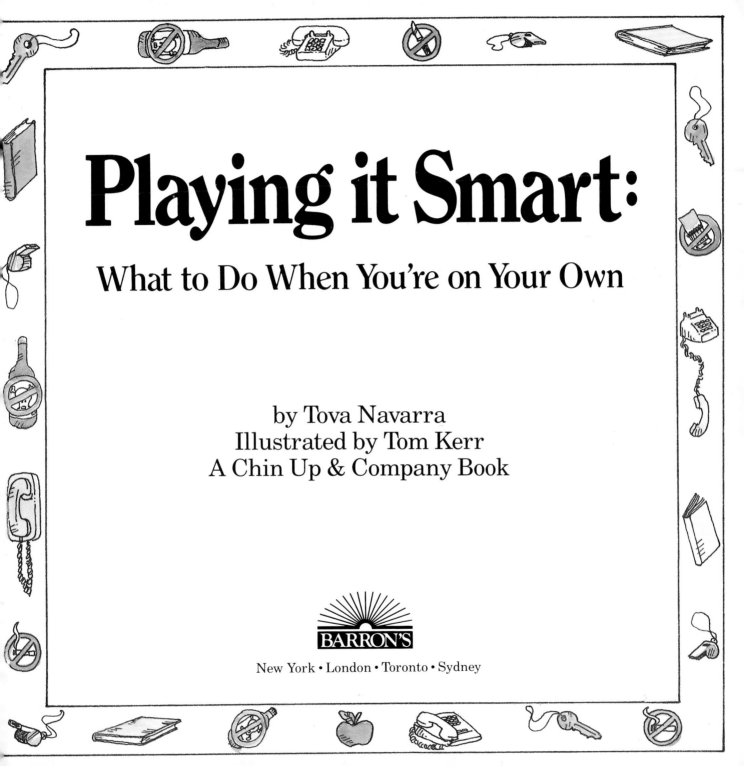

Playing it Smart:

What to Do When You're on Your Own

by Tova Navarra
Illustrated by Tom Kerr
A Chin Up & Company Book

BARRON'S

New York • London • Toronto • Sydney

Published by Barron's Educational Series, Inc.
Text Copyright © 1989 by Tova Navarra.
Illustrations Copyright © 1989 by Tom Kerr.

All inquiries should be addressed to:
Barron's Educational Series, Inc.,
250 Wireless Boulevard
Hauppauge, New York 11788

Library of Congress Catalog Card No. 89-6922
International Standard Book No. 0-8120-6131-4

**Library of Congress Cataloging in Publication
Data**

Navarra, Tova.
    Playing it smart.

    "A Chin up & Company book."
    "What to do when you're on your own"—
    Includes index.
    1. Children—Life skills guides—Juvenile literature.
2. Self-reliance in children—Juvenile literature.
I. Kerr, Tom.   II. Title.
HQ781.N28 1989   640′.83   89-6922
    ISBN 0-8120-6131-4

PRINTED IN HONG KONG

901   4900 9 8 7 6 5 4 3 2

TABLE OF CONTENTS

AUTHOR'S NOTE TO PARENTS

Oh, to be a child again! But children's issues today—peer pressure, broken homes, early sexual activity, molestation, and substance abuse among them—are not the same as they were even a generation ago.

I'd like to help the younger generation figure things out without the agony of trial and error. My challenge, as I saw it, was to create an opportunity for kids to focus on and set in motion their natural intelligence.

No one has all the answers. But the reality is that children do worry about things. While one of my goals was to help parents and caregivers explain touchy topics, another was to offer straightforward advice that kids can read by themselves if they're too shy, as kids often are, to ask questions.

If you read this book with your child, it provides a springboard for communication. As you become more sensitive to what bothers many children, you can discuss situations and give realistic advice *before* there's a problem. Prevention is paramount: children who know some first-aid measures in advance can deal better with a physical crisis; children who understand why people behave certain ways and who have a few stock responses can ward off painful feelings.

You can't be there every moment for your children, but children can open this book anytime for some down-to-earth, friendly information. I hope it gives parents a much-deserved break and steers kids toward a safer and happier childhood.

IF YOU'RE HOME ALONE AND HEAR SCARY NOISES, try to figure out what they could be. You may hear sounds you don't normally notice when other people are around. Do the stairs squeak? Could a tree branch be tapping against the window? Do you know what the furnace switching on or a dripping faucet sounds like?

It's easy to let your imagination get the better of you. If the normal noises still bother you, try turning the TV or radio up loud. It can make you feel less alone and drown out the noises.

If you are sure that the noises aren't normal and could mean danger, leave the house. Go to a neighbor's or friend's house. You can call the police from that other house and let them know what happened.

If you think someone is trying to break in and there's only one way out of the house, try to call the police. Tell them your address so they can find you. Then hide until they get there. Knowing what to do ahead of time can help you feel in control. Remember that most people who break into houses are there to steal things, not to hurt you.

IF YOU GET A CUT OR SCRAPE, the first thing to do is stop the bleeding. Press firmly on the cut with a clean handkerchief or any clean cloth. That should slow the bleeding. If you don't have any cloth, you can use a paper towel or tissues. The important thing is to keep pressing until the bleeding stops. If the cut is still bleeding, cover it and press it again or wrap it firmly in cloth and call someone for help.

If the cut is not too bad and the bleeding has stopped, wash the area very gently with soap and water. Ask Mom or Dad to show you how to use a first-aid cream or spray that will kill the germs. It may sting a little, but that means it is cleaning the cut and will make sure it doesn't get infected. If you have the kind of cut that looks open, cover it with a Band-Aid. Tell Mom or Dad what happened when they get home.

If you learn what to do before you get hurt, it won't seem so bad.

IF YOU GET SOMETHING IN YOUR EYE, go to a sink and turn on the cool water. Splash cool water in your open eye many times. Whatever got in your eye may wash away.

If that doesn't work, stay calm. Don't rub your eye. That could hurt it. Walk slowly to an adult for help.

If there isn't an adult nearby and you think there may be something more serious than a speck of dirt or an eyelash, call 911 for an emergency, or 0 for Operator or the first-aid department in your area. Let Mom or Dad know what happened.

IF YOU SWALLOW SOMETHING
BY ACCIDENT, tell Mom, Dad or an
adult immediately. An adult can
decide what kind of help you need.

If you've swallowed something small
like a toy or penny (and if you are not
choking), stay calm. Dad or Mom will
probably call your doctor to find out
what to do. Sometimes, the doctor will
tell you to wait until the object passes
out of your body when you go to the
bathroom. The doctor may want you to
go to the hospital for X-rays. X-rays
are special pictures that let the doctor
see what's inside of you.

If you or another child swallows
medicine, pills, soap or anything that
could be poison, call the police or the
poison-control number immediately.
Then call Mom or Dad and let them
know what happened. Lots of things
around the house may be poisonous
if you eat or drink them. Even
dishwashing detergent, hand lotion
or shampoo can be poisonous.

Hold on to the bottle or container,
because the doctor will be able to help
you better if he or she knows what
you swallowed. Try to stay as still as
you can until help arrives. If another
child has swallowed something, try to
keep him or her quiet.

You can get electric shocks from an electric cord or wire that is broken or from an electrical appliance. IF YOU GET AN ELECTRIC SHOCK FROM AN APPLIANCE, unplug the cord if you can. Don't touch the plug if the wires are sticking out. If the appliance or wire begins to spark or smoke, get away from it and call the fire department immediately.

Never use anything electrical when your hands are wet or you are near water. Never plug in a hairdryer or the radio while you're in the bathtub or if you're standing in a water puddle on the floor. If a lightning storm begins when you're in a swimming pool or the tub, get out fast and dry off quickly.

If someone else is touching a wire and getting a bad shock, don't touch him or her. You might get shocked, too. You may not hear any yelling or see any sign of trouble, but that doesn't always mean everything is fine. If a wire is causing a shock, the person may not be able to let go of it. Use a stick of wood or a wooden broom handle to push the person away from the wire. Make sure there isn't any metal on the wooden pole because electricity travels through metal very quickly. Electricity doesn't go through wood.

It's a good idea to take the person to a doctor even if he feels okay. Electricity can hurt a person and he might not even feel it.

IF SOMEONE SEEMS TO BE DROWNING, yell and run for help. Don't waste a second. You might be able to get help very quickly.

It is usually not a good idea to jump into the water to try to save someone. When someone is in trouble, he is desperate. He may not be thinking clearly. He could hurt you without even realizing it. Then both of you could be in danger of drowning.

If you are a strong swimmer and have taken life-saving courses, you might try to help the person. If long tree branches or logs are near, you can move them into the water. The drowning person might be able to grab onto them and pull himself out. Or look for something that will float to throw to him. It could be a tire, a large wooden object, life jacket, chair cushion, beach ball or even a raft.

It's very important to swim with other people. That way, someone can go for help if there is any trouble. Always swim in areas protected by lifeguards.

IF SOMEONE HAS FALLEN THROUGH THE ICE, do not go near the hole, even if you think you could grab onto him and help him out. The ice around the hole may be very weak. Both of you could fall through. The best thing to do is yell and run for help.

After you've done that, follow the advice above about throwing the person something to grab onto.

IF YOU TOUCH SOMETHING HOT AND GET BURNED, put the burned part under very cold water or on ice right away. If your finger is burned, open the freezer and put your finger on the ice or some small frozen package. Cold helps your burn heal faster and takes some of the sting from your skin. Sometimes it can prevent a blister from forming.

Wrap the ice in a paper towel and keep dabbing it on your burn (keep it on for one minute, then off for half a minute). Keep doing this for five to ten minutes or until you can get an adult to help you. If your finger turns white, red or very dark, call an adult right away.

If you keep ice on the burn too long, the healthy skin underneath could get too cold and be injured.

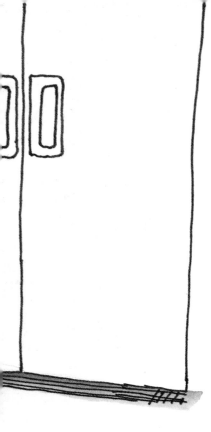

IF YOU ARE ALONE AND START TO CHOKE on a piece of food or an object, run to an adult for help. Don't try to pull it out of your throat. This could push it in further. If no adult is nearby, you should run hard into something about as high or a little higher than your waist (a table, chair or other piece of furniture). This action will push your stomach, force your breath out hard and help force the food out. It is called the Heimlich Maneuver.

Then call someone you trust or the police for help, especially if you feel weak from choking.

Ask your teacher or parents how to do a Heimlich Maneuver for a friend if he or she starts to choke. You may have heard about a boy who saved a little girl's life. He knew how to do the Heimlich Maneuver from watching TV and he used it to stop the girl from choking. Can you imagine how happy he must have felt?

You may help save someone's life if you know what to do ahead of time.

IF YOU ARE HOME ALONE AND A FIRE STARTS, try to be calm and think quickly about what you should do. If flames or smoke are coming from the toaster, TV or other appliances, pull out the plug, but only if you can do it very fast and without getting hurt. Never put water on an electrical fire. Call the fire department. If you don't have the fire department's number handy, call 0 for Operator. Tell the operator there's a fire at your house and make sure you give your address so the firemen can find you. If you have time, close the door where the fire is so the fire doesn't spread so fast.

If a very small fire starts in the frying pan or pot on the stove, turn off the stove. Get a pot lid big enough to cover the pot or pan and put it down over the fire. Stopping air from getting to a fire puts out the flame. Water can put out most fires, but don't throw water on a stove fire. If you don't have a lid, dump a lot of salt or baking soda straight from the carton on the fire. Don't try to fight a fire that's too big to handle. Talk to Mom and Dad about how to decide if a fire is a big or a little one.

If you're in the house and a large fire starts, walk, don't run, out of the house. If smoke starts to fill the room, crawl out of the room quickly. Smoke rises, so you can probably breathe more easily on the floor. If your clothes catch on fire, lie down on the floor and roll back and forth to put out the flames. When you get outside, go to a neighbor's house right away and call the fire department. Don't stop on your way to take anything with you. Don't stop to try to rescue any pets. Just get out of the house as fast as you can. Being safe is the most important thing.

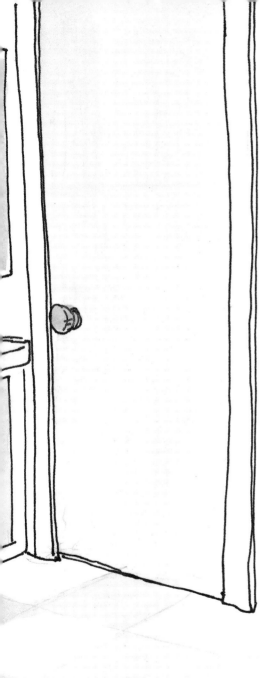

IF YOU ARE ALONE AND HAVE DIARRHEA, A STOMACHACHE, A BAD HEADACHE OR OTHER SICK FEELING, don't take any of the medicine Mom and Dad keep in the house. You might take something that will make you feel worse. Call your parents if you can and ask them what you should do. If you can't reach them, call the adult your parents want you to call for emergencies or a friend's house and ask to speak to his or her Mom or Dad about your problem.

If you still can't reach anyone you know, call your family doctor. Keep the doctor's number by the phone. You can also ask Mom or Dad what to do ahead of time in case of sickness. Knowing what to do ahead of time helps you stay calm and do the best thing.

IF YOU HIT YOUR HEAD AND FEEL A BUMP, put
two ice cubes in a plastic bag and hold it on the bump.
If you don't have ice, take something small out of the
freezer and put it on the bump. If you are outdoors, go
home or to the nearest adult you know. Show the adult
the bump and ask for an icebag to put on it. Let your
parents know what happened as soon as possible.

IF A TOOTH FALLS OUT, rinse your mouth out with cold water. You may bleed a little, but it will stop in just a few minutes. Show the tooth to a grown-up.
And smile! Your baby teeth are making way for your adult teeth.

IF YOU GET TO YOUR HOUSE AND FIND THE DOOR OR WINDOW OPEN, don't go inside. Go immediately to a friend or relative's house. Or go back to the school if it's nearby and there are crossing guards. Ask the adult to call the police. They will come and check your house to make sure a stranger isn't inside and everything is all right.

You can call your Mom or Dad or the adult you're supposed to call in case of an emergency. Carry Mom's and Dad's phone number in your pocket or in a safe place.

IF YOUR NOSE STARTS TO BLEED, sit down and lean forward a little. Don't tilt your head back. Pinch your nostrils closed for a few minutes and breathe through your mouth. That should stop the bleeding. If the bleeding hasn't stopped, do this again for a little longer time. Once the nosebleed is over, try not to blow your nose for a while. If the bleeding won't stop, call or go to an adult for help.

Don't pick at your nose. You might start the bleeding all over again.

IF YOU GET A SPLINTER, see if a piece of splinter is sticking out. If it is, pull it straight out. Clean the spot where the splinter was with soap and water.

If the splinter is not sticking out, leave it alone until you can show it to an adult. If the splinter is very big or a piece of glass, leave it alone and go to an adult for help right away.

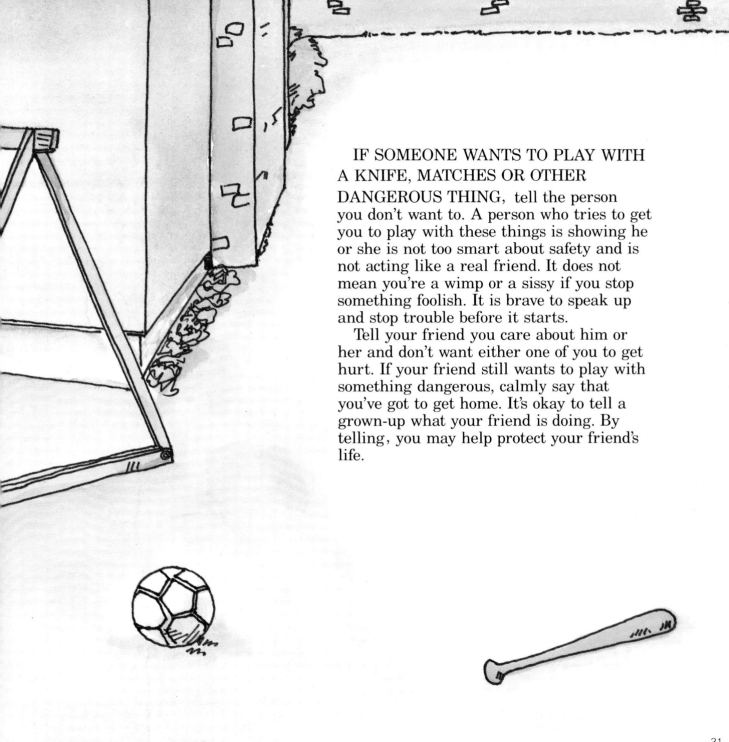

IF SOMEONE WANTS TO PLAY WITH A KNIFE, MATCHES OR OTHER DANGEROUS THING, tell the person you don't want to. A person who tries to get you to play with these things is showing he or she is not too smart about safety and is not acting like a real friend. It does not mean you're a wimp or a sissy if you stop something foolish. It is brave to speak up and stop trouble before it starts.

Tell your friend you care about him or her and don't want either one of you to get hurt. If your friend still wants to play with something dangerous, calmly say that you've got to get home. It's okay to tell a grown-up what your friend is doing. By telling, you may help protect your friend's life.

IF YOU ARE HOME ALONE AT NIGHT AND THE ELECTRICITY GOES OUT, stay where you are if you are comfortable. You may bump into things and hurt yourself if you start moving around in the dark. A blackout usually lasts only a little while, so be patient.

If you have a flashlight, call your parents on the phone or call the person they expect you to call in an emergency. Don't light matches or candles. If you can get to your room easily, get in bed and relax until the lights come back on. You can listen to the radio if it works on batteries.

If you think the lights went out because of a problem in the house, call the police. Maybe you saw sparks fly, heard a strange noise or smelled something burning. Don't use electrical appliances or anything with a plug.

Before a blackout happens, talk to your parents about what you should do.

IF A DOG COMES NEAR YOU, it's important to keep very calm. The dog is probably just curious and wants to sniff you. That's the way a dog gets to know you. If the dog thinks you're not afraid, he'll probably just sniff at you and then go away. Don't shake your hands or make sudden moves. He may look friendly, but you shouldn't try to pet him.

Let the dog walk away from you. Then walk, don't run. Dogs sometimes like to chase moving things.

If a dog tries to bite you, yell and hit him as hard as you can on the nose with a book, a stick or whatever object is nearby. Slowly back away. Go to the nearest place you know for help and tell an adult what happened. Try to remember what the dog looked like so you can tell the police. They should know about the dog so he doesn't hurt or scare anyone else.

IF YOU SPILL SOMETHING, tell Mom or Dad you're sorry and you want to help clean it up. If your parents aren't home, get paper towels or a big towel from the bathroom or kitchen.

Press a dry towel into the wet part to sop up the spill. Pick up the wet towels and put them in the sink. Then get a clean towel. Wet it with cool water and rub it on the area. Don't use soap or any other cleaner in the house. Sometimes soap or other things you use to clean a stain can make it worse. Cool water is the best cleaner.

Tell your parents what happened as soon as one of them gets home. Tell them what you did to help.

IF SOMEONE STOPS YOU AND DEMANDS YOU GIVE HIM MONEY, stay calm. Give him the money. It's not worth getting hurt even if it makes you feel very angry. If the person threatens to hurt you, give him what he wants and let him go his own way. Muggers are usually in a big hurry. Try to remember what the mugger looked like, and as soon as you can, tell a policeman and your parents about what happened.

There are some good rules to follow so you are safer on the streets.

1. Stay in a group of kids when you're outside. Muggers sometimes look for people who are walking alone.

2. If you are walking alone, keep your head up and your eyes open. Try to watch what's going on around you more than usual. Walk a little faster than you usually do. And walk on busy, well-lit streets whenever you can. Dark, lonely streets make it easier for muggers to surprise people.

3. Cross the street if you have a bad feeling about a person coming near you.

4. If you think you are in danger, duck into a store or the post office or someplace where there will be people. If the person follows you, tell someone or start yelling. Muggers do not want to be noticed.

5. If you're going to school or playing outside, don't wear jewelry or your best clothes. If you need to carry money, carry some in the bottom of each sock and a smaller amount in your pocket. That way, you can give the mugger the smaller amount and tell him that's all you have so he'll go away.

Some people who ask you for money are beggars, not muggers. A beggar does not threaten you when he asks for money. Sometimes a beggar may tell you the money is for a good cause, such as saving baby seals or helping hungry people. No matter how kind this person seems or how good his reasons sound, do not stop. Do not give him any money. Try not to even look the beggar in the eye. Just walk away quickly.

Always tell Mom and Dad what happened so they can tell the police and help you in other ways. Always remember that it's much more important to be safe than to hang onto your money or belongings.

IF A STRANGER OFFERS YOU CANDY, A RIDE OR A TOY, don't say anything. Just get away from the person as quickly as you can. No matter how nice the person sounds or what he or she says to you that sounds like fun, just get away. If he says that one of your parents or your brother got hurt and he is going to take you to them, get away. Even if he asks you for some kind of help, get away.

Remember, it's always good to stay with a group of kids when you're outside, at the movies or at a park. It's not a good idea to go to a public bathroom alone. Ask a friend to go with you and both of you keep your eyes open.

If you feel that someone is following you, don't stop to make sure. Go where there are other people as fast as you can. Go into a store or office and ask for help. Try to find out ahead of time where the safe places are in the neighborhood. If there is no one around, yell for help. It may scare the person away.

Always tell your parents if a stranger tried to talk to you. Try to remember what the person looked like and where you were at the time. Talk with Mom and Dad about what you should do if a stranger comes near you again.

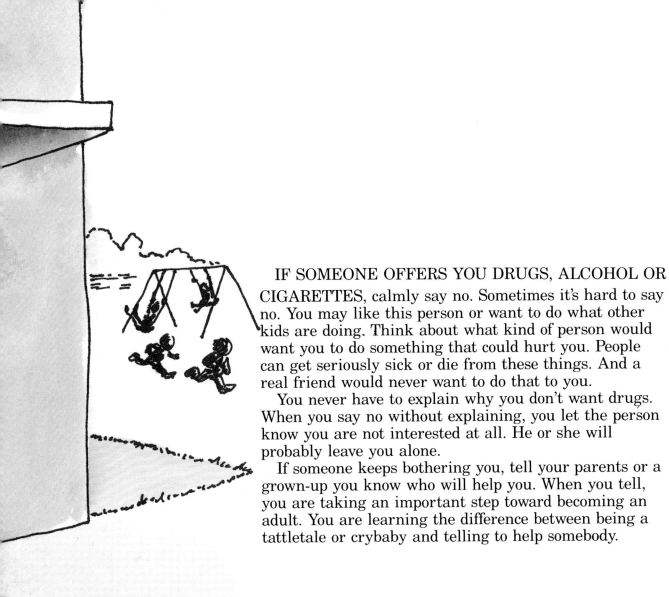

IF SOMEONE OFFERS YOU DRUGS, ALCOHOL OR CIGARETTES, calmly say no. Sometimes it's hard to say no. You may like this person or want to do what other kids are doing. Think about what kind of person would want you to do something that could hurt you. People can get seriously sick or die from these things. And a real friend would never want to do that to you.

You never have to explain why you don't want drugs. When you say no without explaining, you let the person know you are not interested at all. He or she will probably leave you alone.

If someone keeps bothering you, tell your parents or a grown-up you know who will help you. When you tell, you are taking an important step toward becoming an adult. You are learning the difference between being a tattletale or crybaby and telling to help somebody.

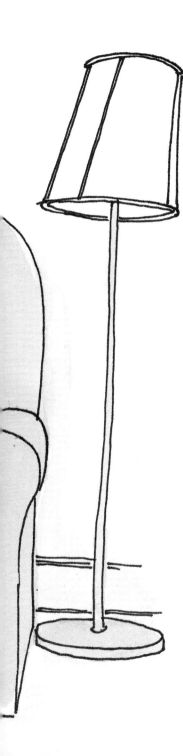

IF SOMEONE TOUCHES YOU IN ANY WAY THAT MAKES YOU FEEL UNCOMFORTABLE, there is more than one thing you can do. First, you can tell the person who touched you that you don't want to be touched like that, even if it is a person you know and like. Tell the person it makes you feel uncomfortable and you don't like it. It is okay to say this and walk away.

Then, tell your Mom or Dad. Tell them the person's name. Show Mom or Dad what part of your body the person touched or if he hurt you. It is important to tell, because people who touch others in private ways need help so they don't do it anymore.

Sometimes it's tough for grown-ups to believe someone they like could do a bad thing, but you should still tell them. You could also tell a teacher or some other grown-up you trust. To trust someone means you believe he or she will help you.

A very important thing to know is that it is not your fault. Some children think they've done something bad and that's why this happened to them. This is not true. It is part of growing up to learn when to say, "Don't do that," and to ask for help.

If no one listens to you, you can call a special free phone number for help. It is 1-800-333-7233. You don't know these people but they are ordinary people like your neighbors who want to make sure you are safe. They volunteer to do this so bad things don't happen to children.

44

A bully is a person who acts tough and pushes others around so he or she can feel important. A bully has personal problems and takes it out on you. That's sad. He or she needs help. Sometimes a bully is a kid who's scared or lonely or abused.

IF SOMEONE BULLIES YOU, speak calmly to him. Bullies want you to get nervous and upset. If you're calm, you may get a bully to listen to you. He might just be trying to get your attention. Tell him you want to be kind and that you want other people to be kind to you, too.

You may want to hit him back or say something. That never helps though. A bully may feel strong by seeing you squirm. He may get a thrill from it and you may only be making him feel bigger when you do these things.

If the bully won't leave you alone or threatens to hurt you, tell your parents, your teachers or the principal. Let them know you need their help. You may not be able to protect yourself from a bully and his gang if they are dangerous. Don't worry about feeling like a baby. You have a right to be safe.

Normal people try to stay away from troublemakers because they don't like to fight. Talk to adults about how to handle the problem of bullies.

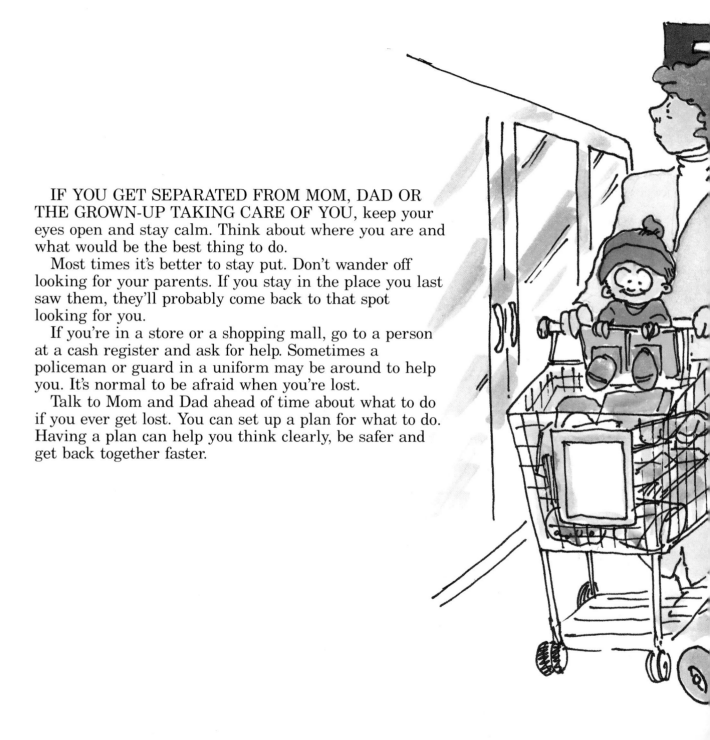

IF YOU GET SEPARATED FROM MOM, DAD OR THE GROWN-UP TAKING CARE OF YOU, keep your eyes open and stay calm. Think about where you are and what would be the best thing to do.

Most times it's better to stay put. Don't wander off looking for your parents. If you stay in the place you last saw them, they'll probably come back to that spot looking for you.

If you're in a store or a shopping mall, go to a person at a cash register and ask for help. Sometimes a policeman or guard in a uniform may be around to help you. It's normal to be afraid when you're lost.

Talk to Mom and Dad ahead of time about what to do if you ever get lost. You can set up a plan for what to do. Having a plan can help you think clearly, be safer and get back together faster.

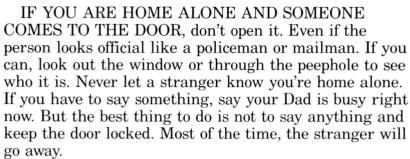

IF YOU ARE HOME ALONE AND SOMEONE COMES TO THE DOOR, don't open it. Even if the person looks official like a policeman or mailman. If you can, look out the window or through the peephole to see who it is. Never let a stranger know you're home alone. If you have to say something, say your Dad is busy right now. But the best thing to do is not to say anything and keep the door locked. Most of the time, the stranger will go away.

If the stranger doesn't go away, call Mom or Dad or a neighbor you trust. Someone may be able to come right over and see that the stranger goes away. If no one you call is in, call the police. Have the number by the phone at all times. Tell them about the stranger and make sure you give your address so they can find you.

IF YOU'RE HOME ALONE AND SOMEONE YOU DON'T KNOW VERY WELL CALLS FOR MOM OR DAD, don't tell them they're not home. Say they can't come to the phone right now.

Then ask the caller for his name and phone number. Write the information down and tell the caller Mom or Dad will call back.

IF YOU REALLY WANT SOMETHING AND DON'T GET IT, you will probably be very disappointed. Being disappointed is a very tough thing, especially if you've prayed, promised to be good or wished very hard. It is hard to know why, but sometimes you are better off if you don't get what you hoped for.

If you pray for something and don't get it, you might want to talk about it with your priest, rabbi or minister. It does not mean you are being ignored or that your prayers aren't good enough. But praying hard for a baby sister or summer camp is not the only reason for praying. Prayers are a way to talk and think about your deep feelings. Some people feel good when they pray.

IF A CLASSMATE WANTS YOU TO CHEAT ON A TEST, cover your paper and say no. Cheating is wrong. The thing about cheating is that, if you help someone with an answer, you are a cheater, too. It doesn't matter whether you gave the answer or asked for it. A person who asks you for answers or asks you to help him see your test paper is not a friend. A real friend would be honest and would want you to be honest.

You could get in trouble at school, too. If you give a friend an answer, you may be helping him or her get a good score on a test, but your friend is learning the bad habit of counting on someone else to bail him out of a tough spot.

Think about what kind of adult a person who cheats may become. Maybe he or she will be dishonest in other ways.

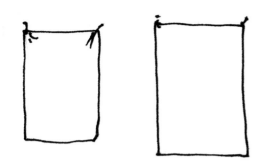

IF YOU NEED HELP WITH YOUR SCHOOLWORK, it's okay to ask for help. You may feel embarrassed and shy about telling your parents or teacher you're having trouble. The work can be very hard for you, but that does not mean you are stupid. You may just need to slow down and concentrate. To concentrate means to think about the work and not think about anything else at that time. It's hard to concentrate if there is a lot of noise going on around you or if your mind is on something else, like a new puppy or band practice.

Sometimes you may feel the teacher is going too fast. And a teacher who *wants* to teach you many things can get jumpy or angry when a student doesn't pay attention. Teachers aren't perfect and students aren't perfect either. After class, you can go to the teacher and say politely, "I know you have a tough job and it's not easy to explain things, but I'd like to hear it one more time."

If you still don't understand, you can say, "Sometimes I'm so confused that I don't know what questions to ask." You should let your teacher know you are trying your best. Perhaps you and your teacher can have a talk and solve the problem. Remember that teachers are supposed to help you learn; it's their job. Most of them decided to be teachers because they want to help you.

One of the best ways to get help is to ask a friend or an older brother or sister to explain what you don't understand.

You should also find out if you're having trouble in school because you can't see or hear well. You may need to have your eyes or ears checked. Sometimes kids have a hard time with schoolwork because of a simple problem that can be solved. Go to the school nurse and find out if your eyes and ears can be checked there. Don't feel embarrassed. Lots of kids need glasses or a tiny hearing aid. The school nurse can probably help you and you'll be happier in school.

IF YOU LOSE A GAME OR FAIL A TEST, you may feel you're not as good as a person who won or did well. You may feel so upset that you want to cry. That's a normal feeling. Nobody likes to do poorly. Plenty of famous people failed at things, but that didn't stop them from trying again and again. All the big baseball stars have struck out. Everyone can make mistakes. The trick is to learn from your mistakes and get yourself back into gear as soon as you can.

It could be that you didn't do all you could have done to make sure you were ready for a test. Or you really didn't play your best game. Next time you might put more effort into getting ready. Then you can feel good that you've put out your best effort.

Take all that energy you're spending feeling sorry for yourself and turn it into energy for practicing or studying more. Think about what you want to be good at and picture yourself doing it. It's important to be positive and to keep trying.

IF YOU ARE SO AFRAID OF BUGS, HIGH PLACES OR SOME OTHER THING THAT IT MAKES YOUR HEART POUND HARD OR MAKES YOU ILL, the best thing to do is start talking about it with your parents, your teacher or a friend. Telling someone can be a big relief and let you know you are not the only one with this kind of problem.

People can feel afraid of many things that can hurt them, like a speeding car or bees flying nearby. Being afraid is healthy when it helps you think of ways to protect yourself.

But sometimes people learn to be afraid of things that really can't hurt them. They become afraid of getting into an elevator, high places or even a neighbor's cat. Sometimes you can teach yourself to get over being afraid of something little by little.

If you fear cats, try looking at cat pictures in a book for just a minute. The next day, look at them for two minutes. Keep going until you can look at them for quite a while without feeling upset. Then try looking at a real cat or going into the same room with one for a short period. Maybe Mom or Dad will go with you so you're not so scared. Eventually, try petting the cat's head for a second. You may find you're not afraid anymore, and the cat is nice and gentle.

Sometimes you can remember something that has happened that made you afraid. Try to figure out what scares you about a thing. It wouldn't make sense to try to pet a bug or snake, but reading interesting things about such creatures may teach you many of them are harmless. Step by step, you can learn not to be *that* scared.

If you are afraid to leave your house, go to school or do things kids normally do, your Mom and Dad may want you to talk things over with a psychologist or other special counselor. A psychologist is a special doctor who helps you get over your unhealthy fears.

Many times you can help yourself. But when you try to solve a problem yourself and still can't do it, you shouldn't be afraid to ask for help from others who care about you. If you think other people will laugh or think you're weak or silly, that's not true. Everyone is afraid of something. It is very grown-up to admit to being afraid of something instead of hiding it.

IF YOU ARE BLAMED FOR SOMETHING YOU DIDN'T DO, speak up. Tell the adults or others involved that you are an honest person and that, even though it may look like you did something bad, you did not. Tell them they've made a mistake. It's normal to feel very angry. You may not even know who is really to blame for doing the bad thing. You may wonder how anyone could believe a bad thing about you, too. You may even feel it is difficult to make the others believe what you're telling them.

That's why it is very important to try to stay clear of trouble. If you play with kids who get into mischief, you're bound to do something mischievous sooner or later. It may even seem okay because your friends are doing it too, but if you go along with them, you are using bad judgment.

WHEN YOU SAY YOU'RE BORED, you are insulting your own imagination. You could probably think of a hundred things to do even if you were alone in an empty room. But if you just wait for something fun to drop in your lap, it probably won't happen.

If you're bored, one of the best things to do is read. Find an interesting book in the library or at home. If it's a storybook, try reading it aloud in a dramatic voice, and imagine you are on stage telling the story to an audience. A book can take you to foreign lands and introduce you to characters you would never otherwise meet. If it's a book that tells you how to do something like make a cake, ask Mom or Dad if you can try the recipe.

Why not try something called brainstorming? That means you and your friends think of many ideas. Some of them will probably be zany, but some could be fun and safe. Then maybe you could do one of the things you've thought of yourselves.

Sometimes a picture book is fun. You can make your own picture book with drawings or cut-outs from old magazines. Try doing an "All About Me" book. Write about the things you do, what you look like and what you think you'll be like when you're grown up. Paste or draw pictures on the pages, too. Then you can make a book cover with two pieces of cardboard that you've decorated. Make some holes down the side of the cardboard covers and all the pages and put string through them.

If you do this project with a friend, you can read each other's book and learn a lot about each other.

IF YOU HAVE A FIGHT WITH YOUR BROTHER OR SISTER, you probably feel very mad. You may even feel like shouting or hitting that person. It's normal to have these feelings at times, but shouting and hitting are NOT the best things to do when you're angry. Instead, when you get mad at someone, count to 10. That will give you time to think.

Words can hurt as badly as being hit. But hurting someone because he's hurt you only makes things worse. Maybe your brother or sister had a tough day or wants to make himself or herself feel strong by attacking you. You can show you are very grown-up by ignoring some nasty comment.

If you are older than your brother or sister, you can be the one who stops the fight. Then you can be proud of yourself for being strong and kind.

IF YOU ARE PUNISHED FOR DOING SOMETHING
WRONG, you may feel very angry and upset. That's
normal. Think carefully about why you were punished.
What should you have done instead? Parents have a lot
to think about. You make their job very tough when you
behave badly. They want to teach you what they think is
right. If you learn what they try to teach you, you will
gain their trust and be able to do many things on your
own. They have to know how you will act when you are
alone.

Sometimes they may feel you don't listen. So sending you to your room or saying you can't watch TV for a week is the only way to get your attention.

If you think you should not have been punished, talk to Mom or Dad about it. Tell them what you think would have been fair and how you could solve the problem together.

And make sure you listen to what your parents and teachers tell you. They want you to grow up to be a happy person who can get along with many kinds of people in the world.

IF YOUR PARENTS ARE HAVING AN ARGUMENT, remember that everybody gets angry sometimes. No one likes loud talking and being angry. But grown-ups do argue once in a while, and it's not your fault.

Stay clear of the argument. Let Mom and Dad be alone so they can settle the problem. Even though arguing makes everyone feel uncomfortable, it means two people are still talking to each other and trying to work out their problems. It is not good when people stop talking to each other and just stay mad. Even people who love each other very much argue. That's because no two people are exactly the same. They have to work to make sure they don't bottle up their feelings. It is never good to hold onto anger.

After a while, you can tell Mom and Dad that when they argue, you feel upset. Most of the time, they will tell you not to worry. Grown-ups have ways of solving their problems.

IF YOU DON'T LIKE BEING THE YOUNGER BROTHER OR SISTER, you're like a lot of other kids. It can be hard to be the youngest, especially when your big brother or sister gets to do something you're not allowed to do yet.

But think of some of the special attention you get just because you're the youngest one. You are lucky to be the youngest because you have a brother or sister you can play with and really share your feelings with. It wasn't so long ago that they were little, too.

It may seem like a long time, but you're only little for a few years. Make a list of all your favorite things. Then make another list of all the things you want to have and do when you're older.

If you think people don't listen to you because you are young, it may be true. There are lots of ways to let someone know what you feel is important. You can tell Mom or Dad that even though you are young, you have ideas. You can add something to their talks at dinner or tell them your opinions, too. An opinion is the way you think about something.

If you feel upset—and sometimes that's natural—talk to Mom or Dad about it. They may understand and help you and your older brother or sister get along better.

IF YOUR PARENTS ARE GETTING A DIVORCE, you may feel very sad and upset. Everything that you know will be changing and it doesn't seem fair. It's a hard time for the whole family. When a Mom and Dad just can't get along with each other, a divorce may help them feel happier. They don't want to feel angry or hurt all the time. Sometimes they have problems that won't go away no matter how hard they try to solve them. Remember that your parents' problem is not your fault. Some kids think they did something to cause the divorce. Or they feel that their parents are angry with them. But most of the time, parents will tell you they love you and will take care of you even if they don't live together. Your Mom will still be your Mom and your Dad will still be your Dad.

Some kids may think that their parents have messed up their lives. It may help to know that your Mom or Dad probably hurt very badly inside. Most grown-ups work very hard to keep their families together, but a split sometimes happens. Also, your parents thought long and hard before making this decision. They may feel it is best even though it hurts.

Talking about your feelings can be a big help. Sharing how you feel with a friend or grown-up you trust may help you get over thinking about the divorce all the time. No matter how bad you feel at first, you will feel better after a while. It may take time.

You may want to visit a library for books that explain more about divorce. The librarian can show you where to find them.

IF A FRIEND DOESN'T WANT TO BE YOUR FRIEND ANYMORE, it can make you feel very sad and alone. This happens to many kids. There are a lot of reasons. Maybe your friend has found another person to have fun with. Maybe the things you used to do together are not what your friend wants to do now. Or maybe it's just tough to see each other because of homework or new activities like volleyball practice.

This friend may not want to be mean to you, but you may feel hurt anyway. Talk with someone you trust about your feelings. You may want to say bad things about your friend, but that never helps and can make you feel worse. Instead, ask someone if he or she ever lost a friend and what you can do about it.

You can also ask someone you haven't been friends with to play with you. That person may turn out to be a lot of fun. Then you'll have a new friend, too.

It's always hard when you like someone more than he or she likes you. Especially when you have been good friends. Just remember that you are special in your own unique way.

Having your own house key is a very grown-up responsibility. IF YOU CARRY YOUR HOUSE KEY, wear it around your neck on a chain or keep it someplace where you'll always have it handy. Make sure you can tuck the key out of sight. That way no one can see it and think you'll be home alone.

Make sure your name and address are not on the key. If you lose it, whoever finds it won't know where you live or be able to get into your house. Always check to make sure you have your key before you leave the house. When you get home, lock the door and put the key in the same place every time so you'll know exactly where to find it the next day.

If you lose your key and can't get into the house, go to the house of an adult you trust. You can call your parents from there and wait until someone gets home to open the door.

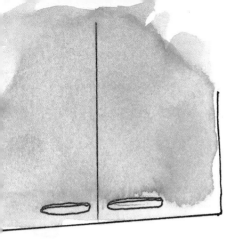

IF YOU BREAK SOMETHING, put on an old pair of gloves. Then carefully put the pieces in a paper bag. Someone may be able to put the pieces back together.

If you break a glass or dish, there may be tiny pieces on the floor. Make sure you have your shoes on. Don't try to pick up tiny pieces with your fingers. Get a dishcloth and gently push the pieces into a bag. If pieces are on the floor, brush them into a bag or dustpan with a broom or handle brush.

If you are afraid you might get cut, leave the broken glass, close the door behind you and let Mom or Dad know what happened. Ask what else you can do to help.

IF SOMEONE YOU LOVE DIES, it is normal to be sad and cry. It probably will help to talk about your feelings or about the person who died. If the person had been sick, think how peaceful the person is now that nothing hurts anymore.

Sometimes you may feel that it is your fault the person died. Maybe you think if you had behaved better or listened more, the person wouldn't have died. This is not true! It is not your fault.

No one likes to think about sickness, accidents or bad things that can happen to people. Even grown-ups get very upset when someone dies. Death is the saddest thing we know. Understanding why someone died is difficult. Usually people don't want to die. When they do, their family and friends may even feel angry. They feel angry because a person they loved cannot come back—no matter what. They have lost someone and it doesn't seem fair. Or they feel afraid that they might die, too.

If you have lost someone who was very special, you should know other people are there to help you. Talking to your priest, minister or rabbi may help you. Maybe you could think about your favorite memories about the person who died. You could share these with your family. You can tell the best things about the person and remember the happy ways this person made you feel.

Remember that life is a special gift. The person who died would want you to be happy and remember good things about him or her.

IF A FRIEND TELLS YOU A SECRET, try to keep it a secret. He or she is trusting you to keep important feelings or events private. It is a very special bond to know a secret and keep it. You may hurt a friend if you tell something personal to others. Think about how bad you'd feel if someone told your secret all over town.

Sometimes someone will tell you a "secret" when she is really afraid to come right out and ask for help. A friend may tell you something troublesome and ask you not to tell anybody. If you feel deep down that keeping this kind of secret could hurt, tell it to a grown-up you trust. That means someone who will understand and really try to help.

Explain to your friend that you care about her. She should know that you will be her friend no matter what and you're going to help with her problem as best you can.

IF YOUR FRIENDS ARE DOING SOMETHING
YOU THINK IS WRONG, tell them to stop or get away
from them. There are times when a game can get out
of hand or when your friends go wild. If they're in your
house and your parents aren't home, things may get
broken and someone may get hurt. Tell everyone to leave.

If they won't listen to you, call an adult you trust
right away and ask for help. If no one is home, go
to a neighbor's house and ask an adult to help you
handle the problem.

Settle ahead of time with your parents the question
of who may play at your house. They'll tell you
whether or not they want you to have company when
they're not home. It's easier to stay out of trouble in the
first place than it is to stop trouble that's already started.

When your friends behave badly, they are showing
they don't have respect for your feelings or things.
They could get you into serious trouble, too. Keep in
mind how terrible you'd feel if someone ripped your
sofa or knocked over your TV set or got mud all over
the place. Kids who do disrespectful things need help.
They have to learn to control themselves.

IF YOU WANT TO GIVE SOMEONE A PRESENT BUT DON'T HAVE ANY MONEY, think about what a gift really is. A gift tells someone you like him and that he is special. When you give a person a present, it should come from your heart. Some presents don't cost any money at all.

You can write Dad a long letter and include your own drawings. You could surprise him by polishing his shoes all shiny. That's one way to say you care enough to give a little bit of yourself.

Sometimes the best gifts are unexpected. You could give someone something of yours even if it isn't new. If you think it is special, there's a good chance the other person will know how much this means to you. Make sure you really want the other person to have it and that he or she would really like it.

Think about writing a poem or giving Mom or Dad 5 tickets for household chores you'll do to help out even more than usual. You'll figure out lots of good things to do.

If you feel embarrassed that a present that doesn't come from a store isn't good enough, think again. People appreciate the thoughtful things you do much more than store-bought presents.

It's not very nice when one of your playmates says something mean to you. Your feelings may get hurt. You may even want to say something mean back. But the grown-up thing to do is much better than that. IF SOMEONE SAYS SOMETHING THAT HURTS YOUR FEELINGS, such as "What an ugly dress," you could say, "Yeah, it is pretty ugly. Maybe I'll send it to The Salvation Army!"

Even if you think you have a nice dress, when you agree with someone who says the mean thing, you let her know she can't hurt your feelings. Chances are she won't get the thrill she was looking for and won't say any more mean things to you. If you keep smiling and make a joke out of it, you are acting strong.

Sometimes people say mean things to make them feel big. That's too bad, because usually that means a person has a low opinion of himself. Saying something mean never helps.

Also, there may be a time when someone says something that hurts your feelings, but he really is your friend and doesn't mean to hurt you. You can say to him, "What you said to me isn't very nice, but I know you are my friend and I forgive you." Someday your friend may have to say the same thing to you.

Have you ever known a person who had more toys than you or had something you wish you had? Or was smarter? Or played basketball better than you? If you ever felt bad that you didn't have something that someone else had, you are like many people. Everyone feels jealous sometimes.

IF YOU FEEL JEALOUS, make a list of all the great things you have had. Maybe you have a soft pillow that's just right. Maybe you have a grandparent who tells you the best stories ever. Or maybe you got to ride a horse or swim at the beach this summer.

Here's something you can do with a friend. Make a list of things you want to have and do when you grow up. Have lots of fun. See how different the lists you come up with are and draw pictures to go with them.

It's nice to have a lot of things, but remember that good things are not always from the store.

IF YOU WOULD RATHER NOT DO CHORES IN THE HOUSE, put on the radio or stereo and just get busy cleaning up. Everyone in your house who's big enough should help Mom and Dad clean up. Mom and Dad need your help with housework because they have a great deal of work to do. Think of everything they do: work at their jobs, go to the supermarket, cook, do laundry, take care of you and a lot more.

Most people would rather be doing something other than cleaning up. It takes time away from other fun things we would rather be doing. But cleaning up is everyone's responsibility. You live in the house, so it is only fair to help out. How about making up a game like "The President is going to be here in an hour"? It can help the job go much faster.

You should know that dirt, dust and clutter can breed germs and bugs. It's a good idea to learn about germs and how you can avoid them. Ask your parents or teacher to explain what germs are. One thing you'll find out is that good old soap and water can keep germs from growing.

It's a good feeling to have everything clean and in good order.

IF SOMEONE WANTS YOU TO TELL A LIE, tell that person you don't lie about things. Lying is like cheating. It can cause you a lot of problems.

Usually a person who lies is trying to get out of a tough situation. It is a bad habit. It might get you out of trouble that one time, but it is a weak thing to do. You may be surprised that your Mom and Dad are proud of you when you tell the truth. They know they can rely on what you tell them. This is the way they grow to trust you and let you do more things on your own.

It's much easier to tell the truth. And you'll feel good about yourself, too. You'd want others to be honest with you, too. Think how terrible you'd feel if a friend told you a lie and you found out.

If you've done something you shouldn't, admit you were wrong even if you know you'll be punished. You get hurt the most by lying. Lying is taking the easy way out. It can make you feel guilty inside and hurt other people.

IF YOUR BABYSITTER DOES SOMETHING YOU THINK IS WRONG, it's important to tell Mom and Dad. Don't think you're being a tattletale.

A babysitter is someone who's supposed to be responsible for you when your parents are out. The babysitter has an important job to do. If he or she invites a friend to your house, drinks alcohol, uses drugs or tells you to do weird things, then that babysitter is not doing his or her job. You could get hurt if your babysitter can't protect you as he or she is supposed to do. You should tell your parents if the babysitter is using something in the house you think he or she shouldn't use or if you have a problem with the babysitter.

Your parents will only know what is going on if you tell them. They hire a babysitter because they want to know you are safe and being taken care of. Both you and your parents will feel better if you are being cared for by someone you trust.

IF YOU SOMETIMES WISH BAD THINGS WOULD HAPPEN TO SOMEONE ELSE, your imagination is at work. Imagining means thinking about things that are not always real. Usually, imagining things is healthy and normal.

Sometimes it can get out of hand . Think about why you want something bad to happen. Has someone hurt your feelings? Or not let you go somewhere you wanted? It may help to think about why the person did what he or she did.

It's hard to look at the other side of things when you're upset. It seems unfair. But you'll be smarter if you try to understand.

Then think about something good and get busy doing something that is fun. If you still feel bothered, tell Mom, Dad or your teacher what's on your mind. He or she may be able to answer your questions and help you not to worry. If you keep it to yourself, you may get more upset. Remember, bad things don't happen just because you imagine them.

IF YOU ARE SICK AND HAVE TO STAY AT HOME, settle in until you feel better. Getting sick is no fun. Most people hate to stay in bed, take medicine and do what the doctor says. You may have to miss a party or something you wanted to do. Most of the time you only have to stay in bed for a couple of days. You can watch your favorite TV shows, have some special things to eat and read an exciting book.

You can also think about getting well. Make a list of things you want to do when you're okay again. That can help your body to feel better.

IF YOU HAVE TO GO TO THE HOSPITAL, ask Mom or Dad to take you there before you have to stay overnight. Then you can see the nurses and see what your room will be like. It won't seem so scary if you ask questions and talk about what will happen when you get to the hospital. Tell Mom and Dad you'd like to know ahead of time.

Sometimes, someone gets hurt or sick and has to be taken to the hospital right away. If this happens to you, try to stay calm. Remember that doctors and nurses at the hospital know what to do to help you and they care about making you better. The hospital is a place where you can get more help than any place else.

It's normal to feel afraid of shots or taking medicine. It may be the first time you've slept away from home or had people examine you.

The important thing to know is that you want to get better, and that may mean being uncomfortable for a while. Find out when your parents can visit you. Talk to a grown-up you trust about your feelings. Sharing your problems can make them seem a little smaller.

IF YOU HAVE TO WEAR BRACES ON YOUR TEETH OR GET GLASSES, you may feel funny about how you look at first. You may think you look silly or ugly, but most of the time that's not true. Many children have to wear braces so their teeth will be straight when they are older. You don't have to wear braces forever. The time you do wear them may seem long, but it will be over soon.

And count all the people who wear glasses! Ask Mom or Dad to help you pick out glasses that look good on your face and will be fun to wear. Remember how important it is to see clearly. Glasses help you do just that. After a while, you'll get used to them, and so will your friends. When you're old enough, you may be able to wear contact lenses.

It's not easy getting used to a different face in the mirror. Braces and glasses are two examples of things that can change the way you look at yourself. Many times the change is for a short time. If the change is permanent, you'll probably feel better for it in the long run. There might even be a time when you think you look funny *without* glasses. You will get used to your new look after a while.

IF THUNDER AND LIGHTNING SCARE YOU, put some cotton in your ears and get busy reading, drawing or doing something you like to do.

To keep safe during a storm, stay indoors and don't use anything electrical or play in water. The electricity in lightning is attracted to water and electrical appliances. Keep windows and doors closed. The telephone runs on electricity, too, so it is a good idea not to use it when there is lightning.

If you do get caught outside in a thunderstorm, try to find shelter. If there are no buildings around, find a low place and stay there. Don't stay under a tree, because high things attract lightning.

A storm is usually just a lot of rain and loud noise. Most times thunder and lightning can't hurt you, but electricity is dangerous and you should be careful when an electrical storm is outside.

IF YOU WORRY ABOUT GETTING A DISEASE OR SOMEONE YOU LOVE GETTING SICK, you might feel better if you knew more about the disease or what could happen. Many times it is a germ that causes disease. Germs can cause serious illnesses like cancer and AIDS, but they can cause minor sicknesses like colds, too.

Ask your school nurse or teacher to explain about germs. She may tell you it's not a good idea to be close to someone with a cold, share your drinking glass or straw or touch someone else's skin when it's bleeding. Germs can spread when you share a piece of food, like an ice cream cone or apple, especially if your mouth touches the food. Germs live everywhere, but you can make it less comfortable for them by keeping yourself and your home clean. Washing your hands a lot is a good idea, too.

If you worry about getting sick, you may want to go to the library. You will be able to find out how people get diseases and what you can do to make sure your body is as healthy and strong as it can be.

Talking to a nurse, your family doctor or a grown-up you trust about how you feel may help you worry less about getting sick.

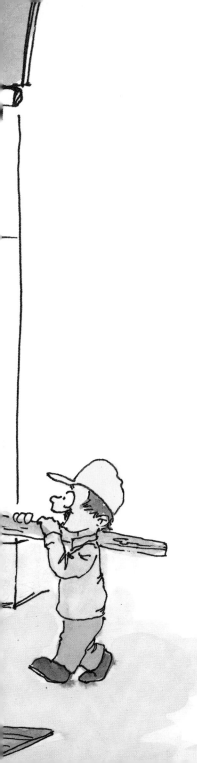

IF YOU HEAR BAD THINGS ABOUT PEOPLE
WHO ARE NOT THE SAME COLOR OR RELIGION
AS YOU, it's hard to just ignore them. Remember,
there are good and bad people no matter what their
skin color, where they came from or to whom they
pray.

If a person says bad things to you about your color
or religion, the best thing to do is walk away. It's sad
when other people try to hurt your feelings because of
these things. They haven't taken the time to find out
what you are like before they make up their minds.
They think they know all about people like you and
don't bother to find out for themselves.

You should feel sorry for people with such small
minds. Think about some of the things they'll never
know. Maybe your Mom makes a cake that only comes
from your parents' country or you can speak two
languages instead of one. You have something no one
else has. No matter what any bully says, he can't take
these things from you.

People say mean things for many reasons. Some
want to make you feel low because you are not the
same as they are or they're afraid of different people.
Your ways or looks, even your food, may seem strange
to them. These people feel threatened by people and
things which are different from them. You are lucky
because you know about two cultures, not just one.
(Culture is the way a person lives and what he or she
believes.) Everyone can learn from each other and
share new thoughts and ways.

It is a bad habit to call people who are different from
you bad names. Remember, if everyone were exactly
the same, the world would be a pretty boring place.
Try to understand why you lash out at a person or a
group. Have you heard bad things about these people?
Have you picked up an attitude from friends or others
that you are better than some groups of people?
Prejudice is a type of hatred that hurts two people.
Mostly, though, it hurts the person who hates because
it closes his mind. That would be a terrible thing to do
to yourself.

103

IF YOU ARE GOING TO MOVE TO A NEW
HOUSE OR NEIGHBORHOOD, you may feel happy
and sad at the same time. You may feel excited because
there will be a new house and neighborhood to get to
know. But you may also feel sad because you have to
leave your friends.

Moving often means saying goodbye to the places
and people you know. But it also means you'll be
learning all about a new place and people. You
can write letters to your best friends about your new
school. Maybe you can send pictures or drawings of the
new place so they know what's going on. They can
write to you and tell you what they're doing.

Sometimes moving can be hard, but it is exciting to
have new experiences. Learning new things is fun. You
may feel shy at first or uncomfortable at being the
"new kid" for a while. But in a little while, you'll get
to know your new teachers and classmates. Soon, you
will be very much at home. And there will be another
"new kid" for you to get to know.

IF YOU HAVE A NIGHTMARE, you wake up scared with your heart pounding. Everyone has nightmares once in a while. A nightmare is like seeing or being in a scary movie while you're asleep. But just remember, it was only a bad dream. It is not real.

Some people believe you can have a nightmare if you eat too late or watch a horror movie or hear something bad on the news. All these things can upset you. Others think nightmares happen when you feel nervous or if something is worrying you. No one knows for sure where nightmares come from, but the best thing you can do is talk about the nightmare with a grown-up you trust. Talking can help you figure out what's bothering you deep down and how to take care of it. A hug from Mom or Dad can make you feel a lot better, too.

IF YOU ANSWER THE TELEPHONE and hear a weird voice or someone saying embarrassing things, don't say anything. Hang up the phone. Tell a grown-up about the call.

Some people have problems they don't know how to solve. They do strange things that even they can't explain sometimes. By not answering them back, you let them know they can't scare or hurt you.

Did you ever feel nervous? Lots of people (even grown-ups) do. IF YOU FEEL NERVOUS, take a slow deep breath in through your nose. Then blow the air out your mouth the way you blow out birthday candles. Do this three or four times. Deep breathing gives you more time and helps you think more clearly.

You can talk to a grown-up or even a close friend about your feeling. Sharing your fears and worries with someone can help you feel better. Remember, everybody needs help at some time, and it's okay to ask for it.

IF YOU FEEL AFRAID OF THE DARK, remember that many other people are afraid, too. Even grown-ups. The dark can't hurt you.

Take some deep breaths and close your eyes. Think how peaceful a dark room is. Maybe you can cuddle your favorite Teddy bear or pat your cat's head.

Maybe you see shapes moving in the dark or imagine creatures under the bed. That is your imagination at work. Maybe the next time a dragon rises up, you could imagine a knight spearing him. You could think about something warm like a bunch of newborn puppies squealing and squirming under your bed.

If you are really scared, you can ask Mom or Dad for a little night light for your room. Think about growing up and not being afraid of the dark anymore. That would be nice.

IF YOU FEEL UPSET BY A MOVIE OR TELEVISION SHOW, talk about your feelings with Mom or Dad or a grown-up you trust. When a movie or TV show is about something gloomy or scary, it's normal to feel gloomy or scared because of it. Shows are supposed to be dramatic. The people who create the shows and the actors playing the parts want everything to seem real and exciting to those who watch.

Remember that even if a show seems real to you, it's usually just a story for entertainment. The actors are not really getting hurt or killed. They're pretending. When some shows do make you feel concerned after they're over, it's okay to ask questions.

Some shows retell true stories. These may make you feel sad, happy or even angry. That's all right. Just talk about those feelings and don't keep them bottled up.

IF YOU FEEL LONELY because your friends are busy and can't spend time with you right now, get involved with an activity on your own. You can read a good book, put together a puzzle or build a model airplane. Sometimes it's wonderful to be by yourself. You can think about things you'd like to do. And sometimes new ideas come to you just because you've had some time to be alone and think about things.

Plenty of children like to be alone and that's okay.

But if you feel too lonely too much of the time, talk about it with your parents. They may help you figure out why you're feeling sad or uncomfortable. They may even suggest ways to make you feel less shy or unaccepted by others. Maybe you could join a club at school and make some new friends. If it's all right with Mom and Dad, call one of your favorite relatives and ask what he or she would do. You can ask your teacher, too. Many people feel lonely at times.

IF YOU HATE TO TAKE A BATH OR WASH, too bad for you. You would probably feel embarrassed if someone told you that you smelled. Or worse, if people didn't want to be around you or talk with you because you were unpleasant to be close to.

You have to get washed every day, like it or not. You have to brush your teeth, wash your face and hands and the rest of your body, and wear clean clothes. Think of how terrible we'd all smell and look if we didn't clean ourselves! Even animals groom themselves and their babies.

Humans do it better, because we know dirt can cause germs and sickness. It's okay to get dirty when you're out playing. But a bath can be fun and relaxing. Ask Mom to help you find a nice smelling soap or bubblebath or shampoo that won't sting if it gets in your eyes.

You can look forward to being old enough to take showers by yourself. Showers and baths will soon feel very good to you and you'll want to be clean all the time.

Have you ever lost a toy or something you liked very much? That happens to everyone. You look everywhere, but you just can't find it. What should you do IF YOU CAN'T FIND SOMETHING YOU LOST?

Maybe Mom, Dad or another person in your house has seen it. Someone may help you look. Or you can make believe you are a detective. A detective is a person who thinks very hard and tries to find answers to things.

Think about everything you did when you last had your favorite thing. Think about where you were in the house with it. Did you take it into the living room? Were you holding it when you were talking on the phone? Could it be under the bed or in a book?

No one likes to lose things, but if you can't find it after a while, it's a good time to think about being more careful. And who knows? That special thing may turn up after a while.

IF YOU DON'T LIKE TO EAT VEGETABLES OR TRY NEW FOODS, you could be missing out on something good. You may be missing the foods that will make you grow, make you stronger and make your brain work better. The foods you eat combine in your body to make it work right. That's called good *nutrition*.

You need to eat foods from four basic food groups. If you want to help your body fight germs and work well, you need vitamins and minerals. You can get them in vegetables like carrots, potatoes, green beans and more.

If you want to help your muscles and bones grow strong, you need to eat protein. You can get protein in meat, fish, eggs and beans.

Dairy products like milk and cheese will work to strengthen your bones and teeth.

You need breads and cereals to help your body clean out your insides, get rid of waste material without any trouble and to give you energy.

Fruit has the vitamins, minerals and natural sugar to keep you on the go. The fiber in fruits helps flush out all your body waste.

It's also important to drink plenty of water (about six glasses a day) to keep your body working properly.

If you're a kid, you probably like hamburgers, french fries and sweets best of all. It's okay to have those foods sometimes, but you need other foods, too. Try tasting different foods. You won't know if you like something until you've tried it. If you taste something you don't like, be polite about it. Nobody likes everything.

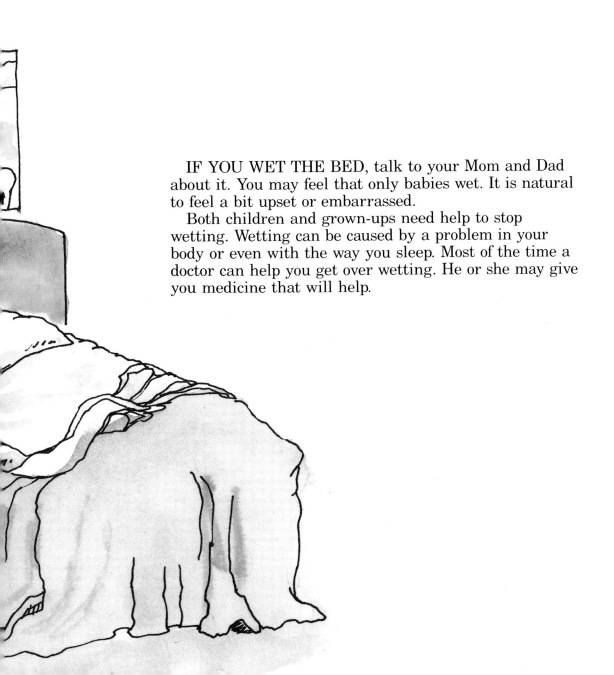

IF YOU WET THE BED, talk to your Mom and Dad about it. You may feel that only babies wet. It is natural to feel a bit upset or embarrassed.

Both children and grown-ups need help to stop wetting. Wetting can be caused by a problem in your body or even with the way you sleep. Most of the time a doctor can help you get over wetting. He or she may give you medicine that will help.

IF YOU PROMISE TO DO SOMETHING, you are saying you will do it. On your honor. A promise is an important decision, so think carefully before you make one.

People rely on what you promise to do. If you promise to help your sister with homework, she is counting on your being there. What if your best friend promised to meet you after school and then didn't show up? You would be very disappointed.

It's important for people to know they can believe you and can rely on your promise. If you promise to call home when you get somewhere and then don't do it, you could cause a lot of worry. That's not a kind thing to do to your Mom or Dad.

When you don't do something you've promised, people think they can't trust you. Sometimes it's impossible to keep a promise. If that happens, you could explain to the person what happened. That's not easy either, but at least the person knows you feel bad about it.

TALKING IT OVER:
Things to Talk About with Mom or Dad

Have you and your family ever made plans to give a birthday party or go on a vacation? If so, you probably have an idea of how important it is to get all the details set ahead of time. That way, each of you knows what to do and the plans can go smoothly. Planning makes everything easier.

If you plan ahead, you'll be able to handle a problem or prevent one from happening. Here is a list of things you should talk over with Mom or Dad.

● Ask your parents when you should call them at work, and whom to call in case of an emergency. Make sure you write the numbers down on the last page of this book. Keep this book or a sheet of paper with important phone numbers by the phone.

● Go over how to use the telephone. Mom and Dad can teach you how to call the police, fire department, first-aid squad, emergency services department or a person they trust to help you when they're not around. Learn how to take and write good messages, too.

- Ask which phone numbers you should learn by heart. In an emergency, you won't have to look them up.
- Find out what your parents expect of you when they're not home. Knowing the house rules ahead of time will help the whole family to cooperate and prevent problems. What are the rules of your house? Can you have friends over when Mom or Dad aren't home? Can you use the oven or other appliances in the kitchen? Make one list for "yes" and one for "no."
- Know your street number, your full name and the name of your town by heart. Always carry identification with you that tells your name, address, home phone number and phone numbers for your parents. That way if anything happens to you, someone can let your Mom or Dad know.
- Ask what you should do if you miss the school bus or arrive too late for an after-school lesson. If you have a plan, chances are you'll be calmer and safer.

Author's Biography—**Tova Navarra**

Tova Navarra is a registered nurse, former teacher and mother of two grown children. A staff writer at *The Asbury Park Press*, Ms. Navarra has written many articles on health, children and family issues. She also writes an internationally syndicated column called "Your Body."

The author of *The New Jersey Shore: A Vanishing Splendor* and *Jim Gary: His Life and Art*, Ms. Navarra is a Seton Hall University and Brookdale Community College graduate who has worked as a psychiatric nurse. She is senior author of *Therapeutic Communication* and has written cover and feature articles for *Today's OR Nurse, Today's Student PT, RN* and other professional journals. She also illustrated *Drugs and Man*, a book for young people.

To my nieces Bianka, Celeste and Christina, my nephew Matthew, Lisa Bogensberger, Jarin and Delil, with love.
Tova

To Mary and Emily who love me just because I'm me.
Tom

Illustrator's Biography—**Tom Kerr**

Fresh from the land down under, Tom Kerr is making his mark in "the States" as an editorial cartoonist and illustrator for a major New Jersey newspaper.

He earned degrees from Williams College and The State College of Victoria (Australia). A self-taught artist, he assembled his portfolio and began his career with freelance and commission assignments.

Mr. Kerr has illustrated several children's books, all published in Australia, including *Getting Started, Getting Started with Color, My Grandfather*, and *Jump into Reading with Gymbaroo*. This is his first book published in the United States.

He is married, has two cats and finished this book amid the wails and rewards of a newborn daughter.

Photography by Steven L. Hersh

INDEX

IMPORTANT PHONE NUMBERS AND INFORMATION

General Emergency: 911*
   *In many towns you can call this number for *any* emergency.
    You should check to see if your town uses this number.
Emergency Services Department:
Police Department:
First-Aid Squad:
Fire Department:
Family Doctor:
Poison Control Center:
Mom's Office:
Dad's Office:
Neighbor Who Could Help:
Relative:
Friend's Mom or Dad Who Could Help: